'When Are You Going to Start a Family?'

My experiences of childlessness and the church

Libby Wilkinson

New Wine

New Wine Press
PO Box 17
Chichester PO20 6YB
England

All Scripture quotations are taken from the HOLY BIBLE, NEW
INTERNATIONAL VERSION. Copyright © 1973,1978,1984 by
International Bible Society. Used by permission.

ISBN: 1 874367 76 0

Typeset by CRB Associates, Reepham, Norfolk
Printed in England by Clays Ltd, St Ives plc

Acknowledgements

I know this may be really boring for those of you who don't know me, but I want to record my thanks to the following people:

Jon – for understanding and sharing everything with me

My family and Jon's family – for loving us and putting up with us through it all

Jackie Bellfield – for all the support and friendship over the past few years

Ruth and Joe Hawkey – for encouraging me to write this book and helping me to believe in myself

The members of Hallwood Parish – for caring for us, praying and being a supportive fellowship

Sue Wicks, Sarah Pinch and Sue Hynes – for their valuable comments and suggestions

Karen Vickers – for the poems; especially *Shattered and Sunshined*

and last, but by no means least . . .

Simon Chesterson – for the gynaecologist jokes.

Contents

Introduction

I decided to write this book after discovering that being childless in the Christian world is like ceasing to exist. There seem to be hundreds of Christian books written every year on the subject of marriage, dozens written on bringing up children or being a good parent and one or two on singleness. There are endless marriage enrichment courses and seminars, and many workshops on good parenting, but I have only ever heard of one course which was devoted to those who are childless.

I have searched through many Christian bookshops and found virtually no books at all on childlessness and infertility – and those I found at first seemed to consist mainly of sentimental, bad poetry, or the miraculous 'the doctors said it wasn't possible' stories. I'm not denigrating those who have experienced a miracle from God in this area, I'm delighted for them; but there is much more to say on the subject. People who don't have miracles need support too and to learn that God has more than they can ever dream of for them – though not necessarily a child. After much searching, I have found a few good books which give various different insights into how Christians can approach the issue of infertility, and these are listed at the back of this book, along with some useful addresses.

Jon and I have taken a few years to understand and accept our situation and I have to say we have done that without the help of the organised church on the whole, though the help and support of individual Christians has been invaluable.

I don't intend to give a great treatise on the causes of and remedies for being childless, but I do hope to share something of our experiences and I trust that what I say may help you to understand what it can be like to be childless in a Christian context.

Like most members of the human race, I have good days and bad days. On the good days, I can thank God for who he is and the way he has led me through my life; I can praise him for the many blessings he has given me. I can get things in perspective. On the bad days, it all seems so unfair: I look at my husband, Jon, who is great with children and wonder whether God thinks we would make good parents (something we are constantly being told by other Christians). I wonder what my life is all about and where I am going. On the bad days, everywhere I go I seem to be confronted by pregnant women or people with babies.

Don't get me wrong, I know that being childless is not the greatest tragedy in the world, but it is important for me to be able to admit sometimes that it hurts. This seems to be difficult for some Christians to accept. In my experience, I have felt pushed into the stiff upper lip attitude – 'your relationship with God should be enough for you, stop making a fuss' – and the opposite (and equally wrong) thought, that it **must** be God's will for Jon and me to have our own children – any acceptance of our situation is taken as a lack of faith. I believe in a God who heals, but I have learned that his ideas of what needs healing in me may well be different to mine.

Before I give the impression that I think all Christians are insensitive or unaware of other people's pain, let me put on record how grateful Jon and I are to those who have stood by us and helped us: those who have listened to us without constantly giving advice; those who have allowed us to have good times and bad without letting this issue dominate; and, most of all, those who have accepted us for who we are, with or without children. I can honestly say that my deepest friendships have been formed through these times and that Jon and I have become much closer as a result of the things that we have shared.

I now realise that God is big enough to deal with whatever we throw at him, and that he understands that it is part of being human to have ups and downs. It's all right to recognise that some of the things that happen to us are not fair, right or God's original intention; we live in a fallen world.

I hope that one thing this book helps to show is that it is possible to live a completely fulfilled life with or without children, whether this happens by choice or force of circumstance. But that doesn't mean that there can't be regrets and sorrow sometimes, whatever our situation. God is sufficient for our every need, but he understands that life is not always easy for us:

> *'Though the fig-tree does not bud and there are no grapes on the vines, ... yet I will rejoice in the Lord, I will be joyful in God my Saviour. The Sovereign Lord is my strength; ... he enables me to go on the heights.'* (Habakkuk 3:17–19)

Chapter 1

Our Story

I have decided not to go into the details of why Jon and I are childless. Ultimately, the reason for our failure to conceive is immaterial for the purposes of this book. What matters is our experiences and how we came to terms with our situation. It's too easy to concentrate on the medical issues and miss the deeper ones, or to imagine that things are different for someone else because their medical situation is slightly different to our own. I suspect that the emotions and problems are similar, whatever the reason for failing to conceive. Please be aware that I am not talking about those who have suffered miscarriages, ectopic pregnancies and stillbirths, or those who have lost children in other ways. I would not assume that I can understand their feelings and pain. I can only speak from the point of view of someone who has never been pregnant, but who would love to have children.

Before I get into the details of the fertility treatment and our experience of coming to terms with childlessness, it may help if I give a bit of background about Jon and me:

We got married when I was twenty-one and Jon was twenty-six. Jon had just finished theological training and was about to start his first curacy. I was straight out of university and had not planned on marrying so young; I was keen to establish my career before thinking about having a family. The first three years of marriage were a real learning time for us both: Jon and I were learning about each other and our marriage relationship, Jon was working hard in a busy city-centre church, and I was getting to grips with the insurance industry.

After three years, Jon was looking for a change and my company were keen for me to move to our head office and extend my experience. The move was a relatively easy one for us, because we both felt that it was time to move on, and Jon found the right job in a parish which was within commuting distance of my head office. At this stage, we both felt that I should think about at least another three years at work. I was still only twenty-four and we felt that there was plenty of time for us to think about having children.

I don't want to give the impression that children were an afterthought for us or unimportant in the scheme of things. We both definitely wanted to have children, but were prepared to wait for what we thought was the right time. This was something that some members of our churches found difficult. There can still be the assumption that once you are married, the children come along very soon afterwards. This is very much at odds with the attitudes that I found at work and amongst my college contemporaries: I would have been considered mad if I had 'given up' my education and career at such a young age. Most women in my situation at work were having children in their thirties rather than their twenties. I believe this is an area where Christian working women can be made to feel very guilty. Are they letting their husband, family, church or even God down if they pursue a career and don't have children, or have children and go back to work? Or are they letting themselves and God down if they don't follow up their talents and gifts in the workplace? Either way, you lose.

So, in the first years of our marriage, we talked about the number of children we might have; we planned for our future. We assumed that when the time came, we would start a family without any problems. Perhaps we took this view because we had been able to plan our lives to a great extent up to this point, and we had no reason to think that having children would be any different.

After six years of marriage, we moved again. Jon took on the responsibility of being the Anglican incumbent in an ecumenical parish in Runcorn, where we still are today. The timing seemed perfect because my company was offering voluntary redundancy packages and we both felt that it was time to think about having children. However, I was unwell before the move and after some medical investigations, we realised that having children might not be plain sailing for us now.

After we moved, we were sent along by our GP to the Reproductive Medicine Unit at a hospital in Manchester – and then the tests began in earnest. This was a very demoralising time for us, as well as a time full of hope. One by one the reasons for infertility were eliminated and we felt very hopeful, whilst at the same time confused because I still wasn't getting pregnant.

The tests and treatment for infertility are much harder on the woman than the man, even if the man is the one who has the infertility problem – though I am not saying that it is easy for men to cope with some of the indignities that they have to go through. There were seemingly endless blood tests, ultrasounds and internal examinations for me, and sperm counts for Jon. There was also the opportunity for counselling, which we didn't take up – I guess we weren't aware of the enormity of what we were taking on – and there were lots of forms to sign. We had to think about some very difficult areas of medical ethics before they became relevant to us; some of them we have never had to face. I'm sure there is scope for Christians to disagree in this area, but we decided that we would not go down the route of using donor eggs or sperm – the whole point of this treatment for us was to have our own baby – and that any frozen embryos we may have would all be used by us; not given to other couples, allowed to die or used for research.

Looking back, we could have done with the help of a counsellor, but we really had no idea of the stress we would be under, or the difficulties we would face. Like most people, we thought we would have a few tests, the doctors would give us a diagnosis, solve the problem and that within a year we would be the proud parents of a bouncing baby (why do we use that phrase?).

We were warned about the relatively low success rates for

fertility treatment, but you convince yourself that it will be different for you. We didn't have the medical problems that some couples face, we were in one of the clinics with a higher than average success rate, we were younger than average and so on.

The doctors didn't give us any false hopes, but they didn't always give us the full story either. I remember going for a routine visit once, part way through a course of treatment. I had been feeling awful; very depressed, no energy, unable to sleep, and Jon was suffering with my mood swings. I had put all this down to being under stress, but I subsequently discovered that these were all side-effects of the drugs I was on. It might have made our lives easier if we had been told this in advance.

One of the reasons for the stress was the fact that very few people knew what was going on – including our families. This is no reflection on them, but rather on the fact that infertility seems to be so hard for people to talk about or deal with. Because we assumed that the treatment was a small hitch, we didn't see the need to tell people – it's not the sort of thing you discuss over coffee in most churches. As time went on, it became more of an issue for us, but also more difficult to mention to others. This eventually led to a real sense of isolation for us. How can you be real with, and feel supported by family and close friends, when you are not sharing the one thing that is dominating your life?

After a year of this, I cracked. I was due to start a new course of treatment involving daily injections, amongst other things. As these were deep intra-muscular injections, I couldn't do them myself (one of my newly-acquired skills) and I had to go to the doctor's every day at the same time to get my jab. I was apprehensive about this and the way that the treatment was taking over my life; and this also coincided with Jon going away for a week. On the Sunday evening, just after he'd gone, I was at church, couldn't handle the way I was feeling and rushed off as soon as the service finished. Fortunately for me, Jackie (who has since become a great friend) noticed that I wasn't at my best and came round a few minutes later to see how I was. I am eternally grateful that she did because of what ultimately came out of that visit, but you'd have to ask her whether she'd do it again. She may have taken on a lot more than she reckoned with at the time.

As we sat there that Sunday evening, I poured out all my feelings and told Jackie about the treatment and how depressed I was with life. She took it all in and, to her credit, didn't say that everything would be all right. She allowed me to stay with my feelings and get them out. This was a new experience for me, as I have spent nearly all my life coping with whatever has crossed my path. Even as a child I didn't share things with my parents, or anyone else for that matter, and this meant that I had become a very self-sufficient person who seemed to sail through life without difficulties. This was very far from the truth, but I couldn't cope with anyone seeing what I thought of as my weak side. It was only when I began to trust Jon that I realised that it was possible to be real with some people.

Over the next few months, it became very important for me to have a safety valve that wasn't Jon. He also needed the help of one of his best friends in the same way. We were both so vulnerable at this time that we could have hurt each other badly – neither of us could be strong enough for the other one, even though we tried very hard.

That last sentence could leave you with the impression that we don't communicate in our marriage. Nothing could be further from the truth. We understand each other much better and know each other inside out as a result of this difficult time. Our love for each other also deepened as we went through this together. The friends that we used as sounding boards were important so that Jon and I didn't get locked into a downward spiral together.

This experience has made me realise that a strong marriage is one where you recognise each other for who you are. It would have been no good for me to expect Jon to meet all my needs at this time – he had needs of his own. We obviously wanted the best for each other and we understood that this involved sharing things with a few other people. The only proviso I would make is that it would have been a mistake to share things with others that I wasn't also sharing with Jon in some way – a marriage partner should be closer than anyone else.

We had various forms of treatment over about three years, starting with relatively low-tech intervention. If you've never been through it, it's hard to describe the emotional ups and downs that each course of treatment brings. Every time you start the treatment, you think that this time might be the one. You plan for the future, choose the godparents, look for all sorts of indicators, physical and otherwise. In short, it can take over your whole life. The disappointment when you realise that another monthly period is on its way can be devastating. There were times when I didn't want to answer the phone just in case it was yet another friend ringing to say that they were pregnant. I couldn't handle other people getting so easily something that I desperately wanted. The ache goes so deep that it affects the whole of your body, soul and spirit. Each time a course of treatment failed, it felt like a bereavement. I know that is very strong language to use, and I don't want to belittle anyone's grief after losing someone they love; but that is the word that comes closest to describing how I felt.

It doesn't help when well-meaning people tell you that they know how you feel, because it took them several months to get pregnant themselves. I used to dream about being able to tell Jon that I was pregnant and seeing the look on his face. Unless you've been through it, you have no idea how much it hurts to give up on those thoughts after years of hoping and clinging on to your dreams. There was a time when I couldn't stop wondering what our children would have been like – their looks, personalities, abilities, likes and dislikes.

After about eighteen months, we were advised to think about trying IVF. Whilst I had heard about it, I didn't really know what was involved. All I had heard was that it had allowed many couples to have children who wouldn't other-wise have succeeded. It seemed an obvious next step and we went into it with high hopes.

I am going to describe the treatment that I had in some detail, because I think that IVF is given a very flattering press, and I believe that there is another side to it – one person I know described the treatment as barbaric and humiliating, and I don't think that is far wrong. I would never say that people shouldn't have IVF treatment – it has given hope (and children) to so many – but I would like to have been given a fuller picture before making a decision.

The IVF procedure starts with the woman's hormonal system being shut down, so that the doctors can control the cycle completely. For me, this involved having a capsule injected under the skin of my stomach. This slowly releases drugs over the next few weeks and means that the woman effectively undergoes the menopause, with all that that entails. After this has been shown to be working, you are given daily injections of hormones to boost egg production. The aim of the exercise is to produce lots of eggs in one go (instead of the usual one) so that they can be removed, fertilised and any subsequent embryos frozen. This can mean that you feel very uncomfortable and painful while the eggs are developing.

My memory is fading a bit, but I think the injections go on for a couple of weeks, and you are also given regular ultrasounds so that the doctors can monitor the state of your ovaries. The reason for this is that there is a danger of Hyper Stimulation Syndrome (HSS), where the ovaries go into over-drive – this syndrome can be dangerous. When the time is right, you are given another injection to release the eggs from your ovaries and then the doctors collect the eggs. I'm not sure exactly how they do this, as I was under general anaesthetic at the time, but I was extremely bruised and sore for a week or so afterwards and felt very lousy. The same day, the man is called in to donate sperm and the eggs are then fertilised.

Up to three of the resulting embryos are then inserted in the woman a couple of days later. In our case, twenty-one eggs were removed from me on the Friday and I was called back in on the Sunday to have three embryos inserted. Of the remaining eggs, eight were not successfully fertilised and ten were frozen for future use. I was told that I was on the borderline of having HSS, but they decided to continue with the implantation process anyway.

I'm sorry if this next statement offends some people's sensibilities; but if you go through this type of treatment, you have to get used to having all sorts of people and all sorts of instruments inside you. Those women who don't like having cervical smears done should think very carefully before having fertility treatment. There have been times when I have been trussed up like a chicken and had various different people poking around inside me for what has seemed like a very long time. Whilst I tried to retain my sense of humour, it is easy to see why women can feel that this type of treatment leaves them violated. I was very fortunate in having understanding and considerate doctors but, even so, I began to dread the internal examinations and treatment.

Having the embryos implanted is by no means the end of the story. You then have to support the embryos by taking hormones in the form of yet more tablets, injections or suppositories. This is because the woman's own system is still shut down. From start to finish the treatment takes weeks and completely takes over your life. If it is unsuccessful, you have to wait at least three months before you can try again, because the woman's body needs time to recover.

I found the whole process very de-personalising. I became a walking (and very uncomfortable) egg-carrier. It felt to me as though I wasn't important as a person, I only mattered because of my capacity as a potential incubator. My own welfare was of no concern, only the embryos mattered. Of course they were very important to me as well, but my sense of self-worth plummeted at this time. That may sound very selfish, and that is probably why I didn't say anything at the time. You become so desperate to be successful that everything else pales into insignificance.

IVF succeeds in producing a pregnancy in about ten percent of cases. Some clinics have substantially better records than others, and the whole thing can feel a bit like a lottery. Treatment can be on the NHS for a limited time if you happen to live in the right part of the country, otherwise it will cost you thousands of pounds. Some GPs will prescribe the drugs and syringes that you need, others will ask you to pay for these yourself. Waiting lists can mean that it is several years before you can start any treatment, unless you can afford to pay for private treatment (private health insurance does not usually cover fertility treatment).

I went through the IVF implantation process three times – each time unsuccessfully. Not all of the frozen embryos could be used, as some of them did not survive the thawing out process.

I found that my feelings towards these embryos, and the ones that did not grow successfully inside me, had to be ambivalent. If I allowed myself to think of them as potential lives, then I was facing a massive loss every time; but to think of them in any other way seemed so uncaring and at odds with reality. What didn't help was the fact that I saw the embryos via a microscope and TV monitor before they were placed inside me: I saw these beginnings of life created from Jon and me and I knew that it was only my ability to nurture them that would make the difference between life and death for them. Inevitably, I saw it as my failure when pregnancy did not follow.

Jon and I have tried very hard not to attribute blame to each other, but there have been times when I have wished myself out of the way so that Jon would be free to have children with someone else. Jon has reassured me that he has never felt this way, but it didn't always take away my feelings of guilt and failure. The way that I resolved this was to say to myself that Jon obviously could not have children on his own, and that we had agreed to put all our eggs in one basket (if you'll pardon the pun) by choosing to marry each other. That commitment implies sacrificing any opportunity in life which would mean breaking the marriage bond.

We used up all our embryos without success, and then had to consider the next step. The hospital offered us some advice, but they would not say what they thought we should do. We could try IVF again or go back to the treatment we had tried before. We decided to make a decision over the next few months, whilst I was recovering from the last IVF treatment.

During this time, Jon was away on a clergy conference and felt that God was saying that we should be thinking about adopting a child. He came back with great excitement as God had also spoken to him on a couple of other issues – something that Jon hadn't anticipated at a diocesan clergy event! We sat in the kitchen, and Jon told me all about it. My reaction was fairly instant and powerful – I burst into tears and couldn't stop crying for ages. Because this was such an important issue, we agreed that we both had to feel that God was calling us in this same direction. I knew that I couldn't let go of all the hopes and dreams that easily, and Jon understood that it would take me some time to come to a decision. This was a very difficult time for both of us. Jon felt that he knew the way forward and he must have been frustrated while he waited for me to catch up with him. I also realised that I mustn't make a decision just to keep Jon happy but had to agree wholeheartedly, or we would be in deep water.

I took a couple of months to come to the conclusion that adoption may be the direction in which God was taking us. We went back to the hospital and told them of our decision. They were very supportive and helpful and said that they would keep our file open for two years, so that we could resume treatment without having to start all over again by being referred by our GP. As we reached the end of the consultation, it really hit home that we were taking an enormous step and I recognised exactly what we were leaving behind. I managed to get out of the waiting room before I dissolved into tears, and then I wept for the rest of the morning.

Once the initial anguish was over, though, I realised just how relieved I was that we had made the decision and got off the treadmill of treatment. I know it's a bit of a cliché, but it was as though a great weight had been lifted from me. It became clear to me just how much the fertility treatment had taken over my life, and I was glad to stop. Having said this, it was important for me to give the treatment my best shot, otherwise I may have been left with the thought, 'if only we'd tried once more...' Life is too short to have those regrets, though I know lots of people have them for all sorts of reasons.

We then started to think about adoption and contacting various agencies. We had no idea where to start and who we should turn to for advice. In the end, we obtained a leaflet listing all the major adoption agencies in the country and we started writing to those who were in our area. We got very little response to start with. One agency was so rude, patronising and condescending that we refused to deal with them any more; others had closed down or were outside our area. The only agency we got a very positive response from was our local social services, much to my surprise. One of the family finding team came round to see us and spent three hours talking and listening to us. He talked of the need to allow time to grieve for the family we were not now going to have, he explained the adoption procedure in some detail and answered all our questions honestly and openly. He advised taking a few months to think things over and then to get back in touch if we were sure that adoption was the route for us. We did just that.

The approval procedure for adoption is long and thorough, and that is the way it should be. The vast majority of children placed for adoption now are older than babies and most have had a difficult start in life. They need more than just well-meaning amateurs who are looking to fulfil their own needs. We had to attend a series of evening meetings to look at parenting issues, the background to fostering and adoption, social and medical issues; and we also had talks from the child protection team and an educational psychologist. As well as this, we were given our own social worker who had to do a home study report on us. Her job was to assess whether we would be suitable candidates for being adoptive parents. She looked into our backgrounds and our current lifestyle in great detail and we also had to undergo medical and police checks. The whole process takes several months and leaves no stone unturned. At the end of it all, we were good friends with Joy, our social worker, and we were approved for adoption. Then the real waiting started.

There are more people waiting to adopt than there are children needing homes, so inevitably there is a wait involved. The only good thing is that you don't start at the end of the queue. The child's welfare should always be given priority, so you may be matched with the first child you apply for, if they think that you offer the best chance for that child. On the other hand, this means that there are no guarantees about when it will be your turn, and that is where Jon and I are at the moment – waiting to be matched, with no idea of whether we will have a child in two months or two years. Whilst this makes it difficult to plan anything in advance, we are coping quite well with the wait – we are both so sure that this is where God wants us to be. It's not easy to be told that you've just missed out on being chosen for a particular child, but we know that God has the right child or children for us and we will wait for his timing.

We have found God to be a real strength for us at times when the adoption selection procedures seem unfair or unwieldy. I remember a picture God gave me when I was very low and felt that I just couldn't cope with any more emotional upheaval: I saw a picture of a heart which had been ripped down the middle, but it wasn't falling apart. There were two hands cradling it and holding it together, and a voice very clearly said to me, 'I'm big enough to deal with all this.'

Jon reacted to the same situation in a different way. He was angry with some of those who were making decisions about us and he wanted to protest and take action. Around this time, he was in a service where one of the readings was from Romans 12. A few of the verses leapt out at him, and as this was a meditative service, there were ten minutes of silence after the reading. This gave him plenty of time to think about the significance of what he had heard and read. The verses which God showed him were these:

'Be joyful in hope, patient in affliction, faithful in prayer.'
(Romans 12:12)

'Bless those who persecute you; bless and do not curse.'
(Romans 12:14)

Jon realised that these verses were a neat summary of the way that God wanted us to be during this waiting time. God understands that we don't always find it easy, and he cares about how we feel.

Experiences like this help us to leave the future in God's hands. He knows what he's doing and he can handle things so much better than us.

Chapter 2

What About the Bible?

I could never be described as a biblical scholar, and so I am approaching this chapter with some trepidation. In the past, I have not looked closely at what the Bible has to say on the issue of infertility, perhaps because I thought I might not like what I found. I have gathered that barrenness was seen, particularly in the Old Testament, as a sign of God's disfavour or the result of sin (see Exodus 23:26 and Deuteronomy 7:14). I want to consider this now, along with the stories of some childless people in the Bible.

First of all, I want to look at the word 'barren', which a lot of translations use. Jon assures me that it is a good translation of the Greek word, but I do have some difficulty with it – not on theological grounds, but because of the connotations of the word. Current dictionaries define the word 'barren' as unproductive, dull, devoid of features and sterile. It is interesting to see that some of the newer Bible translations try not to give such negative overtones because they use the words 'childless' or 'never able to have children'. Words do change their meaning over time and 'barren' seems to me to be such a desolate word to use. Consequently, I don't use it.

There are lots of examples of people who are childless in the Bible, but I have only come across one person who remained that way throughout their life. That person was Michal, Saul's daughter and David's wife who *'despised him in her heart'* (2 Samuel 6:16) and mocked him for dancing before the Lord. She had no children to the day of her death (2 Samuel 6:23). The implication is that this was a direct result of her despising her husband and not honouring what he was doing for God. In every other situation that I have found in the Bible, the childless person or couple go on to have at least one child, sometimes many more.

The simplistic conclusion to draw from this is that people are only childless throughout life if they have offended God in some way or do not have a right attitude to their marriage partner. I think the issue for Michal was more to do with her lack of repentance and hardness of heart. It does seem though that this specific incident caused Michal's inability to bear children. This is a very serious consequence and one that should make us all stop and think about the effects of some of our own ill-judged actions. Our attitudes and actions matter. They make a difference to our lives and the lives of those around us.

I don't think, however, that it then follows that **all** childless people should scour their past to discover the issue that is stopping them from bearing children. It is a useful exercise for all Christians to examine their lives to see if they have deliberately or inadvertently placed barriers between themselves and God, but this will not automatically bring about conception for all infertile couples. The Bible is clear that this is not always the reason for childlessness: Elizabeth and Zechariah were childless, but Luke describes them as upright in the sight of the Lord and those who lived blameless lives (Luke 1:6). Their son, John the Baptist, is not given to them as a result of repentance for sins committed, but rather to fulfil God's purposes.

We are not told why Elizabeth and Zechariah had no children, we're just told that Elizabeth was barren (NIV translation) and that they were both old. Perhaps there was no specific cause of Elizabeth's inability to bear children, or it just wasn't relevant to what Luke was saying. Society had obviously made its feelings known, though, in that Elizabeth talks of the Lord taking away her disgrace by giving her a child (Luke 1:25). Do we still do that to people today? Do we assume that there must be some problem that needs to be sorted out, or some past failing that God is taking revenge for?

I think that we need to keep a sense of balance here. Yes, the way we behave has consequences for our lives and, if we come to God in repentance, barriers will be broken down and problems will be resolved. Having said that, there came a point for me where I had to stop beating myself over the head, trying to find the key in my life that would unlock the door to having children. If we honestly come before God and ask him to show us anything in our life that is hindering us, then I believe he will do just that. He doesn't try and make it difficult for us and he doesn't withhold his compassion just because we can be slow on the uptake.

Sometimes in the Bible, we see that God's compassion is aroused by the heartfelt cries of those in pain, and that brings me to Hannah. I can really relate to Hannah (or, at least, I thought I could until I discovered she ended up being the mother of six). She was desperate for children. Her husband's other wife, Peninnah, had children but *'the Lord had closed Hannah's womb'* (1 Samuel 1:5). Peninnah used to make life a misery for Hannah, by pointing out year after year, how inadequate she was. Hannah goes to the temple and pours out her heart to God *'in bitterness of soul'* (1 Samuel 1:10) and I'm sure that the words 'it's not fair' must have crossed her lips. God hears her cries and her promise to dedicate her child to him, and he gives her Samuel. Hannah keeps her promise by sending Samuel to Eli in the temple when he is still very young. Eli blesses Elkanah and Hannah and, over the years, the Lord is gracious to Hannah and she has five more children (1 Samuel 2:21).

I can understand where Hannah is coming from, because I have felt the bitterness, pain and anger that is described in this passage from 1 Samuel. I have found it difficult to deal with my feelings when I have heard about family, friends or acquaintances who have become pregnant. Hannah must have had similar thoughts about Peninnah; particularly because of the way that she was treated by Peninnah. I would not want to claim that I have ever been told how inadequate and pathetic I am by other women, but some people have left me feeling that way because of their unthinking remarks.

Rachel, wife of Jacob, cried out that she would rather die than live without children (Genesis 30:1). Her older sister Leah had sons by Jacob, and the writer of Genesis suggests that this is because Leah was not loved by her husband – just look at the names Leah gives her first two children: Reuben means 'the Lord has seen my misery', and Simeon is named because 'the Lord has heard that I am not loved'. Rachel had the love of her husband, but no children. Eventually, *'God remembered Rachel and listened to her'* (Genesis 30:22) and she gave birth to Joseph, but then later she died giving birth to her second son, Benjamin.

Do the experiences of Hannah and Rachel mean that you only have to ask often enough, or with sufficient passion, and God will grant your request? I acted as though this were true for a while. I could not believe that God would want me to remain childless, and so I would keep asking God, sometimes very bitterly, what did he think he was playing at? For how long did he want me to learn patience? I didn't always see the irony in that last question.

Hannah's story, and those of Rachel and Leah, show us that God is compassionate and gracious, but I think that they also show that God is sovereign. I don't understand why God sometimes says yes, but other times he says no. What I do know is that he shares the pain of people like Hannah, and he brings her to a place where she can say that *'her heart rejoices in the Lord'* (1 Samuel 2:1). I don't think that this is just because God has given her a child – her prayer majors on the character and sovereignty of God, not herself (see 1 Samuel 2:6–8), and how he has power over even the most basic facts of life. There are overtones of the Magnificat here, too.

Sarah, the wife of Abraham, was promised a son at the age of ninety. She laughed at the idea (Genesis 18:12), but Isaac was duly born within a year, as God had promised. Sarah is described as the one with the fertility problem, as Hagar had already borne a son to Abraham. Sarah was obviously highly sceptical of becoming a mother at her great age, but in spite of her initial reaction, she is included in Hebrews 11 as a person who lived by faith:

> *'...even Sarah, who was past age, was enabled to bear*
> *children because she considered him faithful who had made*
> *the promise.'* (Hebrews 11:11, NIV footnote)

I think the crucial thing here is that Sarah and Abraham knew God's voice and the fact that he could be trusted to keep his promise. If you are ever praying with or talking to someone who longs for children, please don't ever tell them that God will give them a child, unless you are completely one hundred percent sure that you have heard God specifically and correctly. You may cause a lot more problems than you realise, if you give a word that you think is encouraging but it then doesn't actually happen. I'm not saying that praying for children or the healing of infertility is inappropriate, far from it – but please let God be God. Your job as a prayer minister is not to make the childless person feel better or to give them false hope; it is to be a channel of God's love to them, whatever that means in their particular situation.

When I have allowed people to pray with me on this subject, it has always been with some nervousness unless I have known the person well. All too often, it feels as though I am not hearing God speaking, but the preconceived ideas and expectations of the person praying. This can place you in a no-win situation: if you don't receive prayer, are you refusing to accept what God may have for you? Are you missing out on the one opportunity that might change your life? On the other hand, if you do ask for prayer, you may only be opening your vulnerable self up to yet more hurt and disappointment.

If this puts you off praying for the childless because you are unsure how to pray and want to avoid causing hurt, then you would probably be fine. It's the people who think that they have all the answers that are the problem. Always remember that you are praying for a person and not for a problem. Let God minister to them and don't get in the way. Ask God to do the things that he has promised in the Bible; ask him to bless his children and to give them what is best for them. If you feel that God is showing you that there is an issue to be dealt with, then mention it gently; but don't force the issue, and try to be aware of your own motives and judgements when doing this. Don't make any assumptions about their medical condition or past behaviour, but don't ask for details that the person doesn't want to give either – God will show you anything that you need to know. Above all, allow the person you are praying for to retain their dignity and sense of worth in the eyes of God. A lot of childless people have problems with low self-esteem, and they do not need it reinforcing. They need to hear about God's love and their worth in his eyes.

When Elisha stays with a Shunammite couple, he wants to return their hospitality by doing something for them (2 Kings 4:8–37). His servant tells Elisha that they have no son and so Elisha calls the Shunammite woman and tells her that she will have a son in the next year. This poor woman has obviously suffered at the hands of people telling her things like this in the past and she responds by saying 'No, my lord ... Don't mislead your servant, O man of God' (2 Kings 4:16b). She doesn't want to spend yet more time coping with the disappointment of unfulfilled expectations. As Elisha really had heard God correctly, though, there was no problem and the woman gave birth to a son about a year later.

Manoah's wife is described in Judges 13:2 as a woman who was sterile and had remained childless. We know very little else about her, except that she became the mother of Samson. She was visited by an angel who told her that her son was to be the one who would begin the deliverance of the Israelites from the hands of the Philistines. She was a woman of faith, who accepted the words of the angel more easily than her husband. The important thing here, I think, is that Manoah and his wife could do nothing about their childlessness. God does not ask them to jump through any hoops or resolve any past problems. They are given a child, again, to fulfil God's purposes, and not because of anything they have or haven't done.

So, looking at biblical examples, we can say that some people are childless because of their behaviour and attitude towards God (namely, Michal), others are not. Childlessness does not definitely mean God's disfavour or past unresolved sin. I'm not sure what other conclusions to draw, except that God is compassionate to all these women and doesn't demand anything from them. He treats each of them as they need to be treated.

One thing that really struck me whilst reading these stories, was that the cause of the childlessness always seemed to be laid at the woman's door. Is this a cultural response or a matter of fact? Nowadays, male infertility accounts for about one third of cases of childlessness (a similar proportion to female infertility), and there is no reason to suppose that things were any different in biblical times. Having said that, Sarah, Rachel and Hannah had husbands who had children by other women, though Abraham came to fatherhood very late in life. Of the other cases considered, Zechariah had no children, but the cause of infertility is placed with Elizabeth. Similarly with Manoah's wife – she is the one described as sterile and childless. It may simply be that their knowledge of human biology was lacking and there was no precise way of telling if a man was infertile, but it was obvious if a woman had not given birth to a child.

It is still difficult in our culture to relate this issue to men. Very often, it is seen as a woman's issue, even though it is almost as common for the male to be infertile or sub-fertile. This means that the man can get left out in dealing with, or discussing the problem of childlessness. I am aware that some people are very concerned about me and my feelings, but fewer give any thought as to how Jon may feel in all this – whether he may find it very difficult to baptise babies or deal with children as part of his job. Men are just meant to cope in our society.

How do childless men relate to these Bible examples? Does the Bible have anything to say to them? I have to say that I can find very little on this specific subject. Another thing that struck me was that there is very little about this subject in Jesus' life or in the New Testament writings. There is no recorded healing of infertility by Jesus, although gynaecological issues are mentioned.

Those of you who are on the ball will be saying that one

aspect I haven't really considered is the issue of whether childlessness is a sign of a curse. Starting in Genesis, we see that it is God's intention for us to reproduce and subdue the earth (Genesis 1:28). Things started to go wrong when we rebelled against God, and that's when infertility must have come on the scene, along with lots of other things that God did not want for us. We must always remember that we live in a fallen world and, as Christians, we are just as much subject to its effects as everyone else. That doesn't mean, though, that we have to accept sickness or anything else in a fatalistic way. We have a God who has intervened, intervenes now and who will intervene in the future.

Deuteronomy 28 lists the blessings and curses that the Israelites can expect, depending on whether they obey God and follow all his commands. Included in these lists is fertility (or the lack of it), described here as the fruit of the womb. This list outlines that childlessness (and lack of reproductiveness in its broadest sense) is one of the consequences of disobedience and rebellion against God; along with poverty, defeat, sickness, oppression, failure, family breakdown, humiliation and God's disfavour. These consequences affect not only those who disobey God, but also those around them and their family line.

The Bible is clear that blessings and curses are part and parcel of lives that involve the spiritual realm, and our behaviour can determine how we are affected by them – although it would be wrong to say that these things are always self-imposed. In Deuteronomy 30, Joshua gives the Israelites an ultimatum to choose blessings or curses, life or death. They are not just victims of circumstance; they can have an influence on their own lives by the decisions they make. By choosing to obey God and all his commands, they can ensure God's blessing.

I think that an in-depth analysis of blessings and curses is outside the scope of this book, but if you are interested in looking deeper, I would recommend a book such as *Blessing or Curse: You Can Choose* by Derek Prince. The point I want to make here is that it may be, for some people, that a curse on them or their family is influencing their ability to have children. If that is the case, it does not mean that there is no hope. In Jesus, we have the perfect sacrifice who became a curse so that we may receive blessing.

> *'Christ redeemed us from the curse of the law by becoming a curse for us, for it is written: "Cursed is everyone who is hung on a tree." He redeemed us in order that the blessing given to Abraham might come to the Gentiles through Christ Jesus, so that by faith we might receive the promise of the Spirit.'*
> (Galatians 3:13–14)

This 'blessing of Abraham' refers back to the lists in Deuteronomy 28. By dying for us on the cross, Jesus broke the power of curses and gave us access to the blessings of God. Our problems will not be solved, though, if we are not listening to God, or being sensitive to the leading of the Holy Spirit. We may seek prosperity (one of the blessings listed in Deuteronomy 28), but God's first priority with us may be something completely different. The fact that God has the power to break curses and to institute blessings does not make him into a vending machine that hands out whatever we ask for. If we go on asking for one thing when God wants another for us, we may end up with neither.

So, it may well be helpful for childless couples to explore this avenue of possible curses and their effects, but I would not want to over-emphasise its importance. It is not the whole answer.

What comes across to me from the Bible as a whole, is the immense love of God and his desire for us to be in relationship with him. He made us all individuals and we are intrinsically valuable to him. Let's use what he has given us in the Bible to help, sustain and release people; but not to give simplistic answers to complicated problems. We're not going to know the whole story while still in this imperfect world:

'The secret things belong to the Lord our God, but the things revealed belong to us ..., that we may follow all the words of this law.' (Deuteronomy 29:29)

Chapter 3

What Are the Facts?

One in six couples experiences some difficulty in conceiving. One in ten couples seeks medical help or advice because of this difficulty. This means that in your average home group there will be someone who has personal experience of this problem. Most churches will have at least a handful of people in this situation, or those who have been through it in the past. Whilst a lot of them will go on to have their own children eventually, some will not. When I took the step of telling the church about our situation, I was surprised by the number of people who then shared their experiences with me. Some of them had endured years of hoping and trying, but had never felt able to say anything about it before. Most of them now have children, but they could relate all too well to the feelings that I was talking about.

Why is infertility such a hidden problem? Why did these people feel that they couldn't talk about their experiences and struggles with their church friends (or anyone else, I suspect)? At least part of the reason is that there is a fear that people won't understand what is involved, or that they will jump to conclusions. There is still a taboo about admitting that you can't have children. Telling people that you are infertile produces a similar sort of reaction to the one that I used to get at work when I told people that my husband was a vicar – all of a sudden, some people don't know what to say to you, or they apologise for the things they have already said. Straightaway, you cease to be a person and become a category.

In this chapter, I want to try to lay to rest some of the

myths and assumptions about infertility. I hope to give you some idea of the difficulties and uncertainties that childless people have to deal with, and I trust that those of you who are fortunate enough never to have thought about this subject will gain a degree of understanding.

One fact that can be difficult to grasp is that there are very few certainties in the fertility game. Even if both partners are fertile, there is no guarantee of conceiving at a particular time. If either or both partners are sub-fertile, then it just means that the percentage chance of conceiving is reduced, but not eliminated. In a sense, the probabilities matter very little when you're in the situation yourself, you either get pregnant or you don't.

You may be in the fifteen percent or so of couples where no obvious cause for infertility can be found. This seems to be at odds with how we see the world. We always want to search for the cause. There must be a reason for the infertility, or conception would take place. Unfortunately, sometimes the world doesn't work the way we think it should – a couple who are both apparently fertile sometimes just don't conceive.

It can be difficult to handle such an uncertain situation. If you are told that a course of treatment has a twenty-five percent chance of success, it is difficult not to assume that you will have conceived by the fourth time of trying. Unfortunately, probability theory doesn't work like this and some people who seem to have a reasonable chance of conceiving, just don't.

Modern medical advances mean that people who would have been completely infertile in the past now have a chance to become parents. This can be a positive thing for these couples, but it can also mean that it becomes very difficult to come to terms with the fact that you may never have children; because there is always one more thing you can try, there are always new techniques and procedures. It can be very difficult to tear yourself away from fertility treatment. I heard one woman describe how she felt that she had an unborn child in her head, and she knew that she had to do everything she could to allow this child to come into existence. She considered that she would have been betraying this child if she hadn't put herself through everything possible to try and conceive. There can be a real desperation and need to continue with treatment, even against all the odds. Some people continue with fertility treatment for as long as ten or fifteen years. Speaking from my own experience, I don't know how they do it.

Infertility is a growing problem. Some research suggests that sperm counts are declining. This is not a conclusion that is universally accepted, but there is some evidence that more men are falling into the sub-fertile category; where it is more difficult, but still possible, for them to father children. Sexually transmitted diseases (some of which can cause infertility) are on the increase – particularly chlamydia, a disease with few initial symptoms, but which can cause pelvic inflammatory disease, and subsequently infertility. Abortions can cause inflammation of the fallopian tubes, or surgery can produce adhesions which may block the fallopian tubes and lead to a woman being unable to conceive. A society which has liberal sexual values and which allows abortions virtually on demand will be a society where infertility is an issue. Unfortunately, this describes our current society.

Infertility is recognised by the World Health Organisation as a medical condition, but some health authorities in this country do not take this line, and consequently they will not fund any treatment. They say that infertility is not an illness and so treatment should not be provided on the NHS; or very restrictive patient criteria are imposed so that only a few couples qualify for treatment. If you have any children at all, whether from a previous relationship or not, you are much less likely to qualify. Your age and personal circumstances can also count against you. Some health authorities will only offer certain types of treatment – ovulation induction treatments and fallopian tube surgery may be offered but not IVF, for example. Twenty-five percent of health authorities do not fund IVF at all, others will fund only one or two cycles. This can mean that inappropriate treatment is offered, because the best treatment for the couple concerned is not available on the NHS. This is a waste of time for the couple and a waste of NHS resources. I have heard of cases where the woman has been given drugs to promote ovulation without any checks being made to see that her fallopian tubes are clear (one of the major causes of female infertility).

This all probably comes out of the need to ration resources rather than any dismissal of infertility as a real problem, but it does mean that a couple who need fertility treatment not only have to deal with the implications of the diagnosis and treatment – pretty mind-blowing in themselves – but they usually also have to decide whether they can afford to take the steps necessary for them to have a chance of conceiving. Seventy-five percent of couples have to pay for some or all of their treatment, and on average they spend between £1,000 and £4,000.

Even if you are lucky enough to be given treatment on the NHS, waiting lists are a major problem. You will take time to be referred by your GP, especially if you are unsure about how long you have been trying to conceive. Once at the Reproductive Medicine or Assisted Conception Unit, you may well have to wait before being considered for the IVF waiting list. It can all seem never-ending.

As well as the practical difficulties in obtaining fertility treatment, there is all the emotional upheaval. Nine out of ten people who are in this position suffer from depression, isolation and frustration. One in five infertile people have thought about committing suicide whilst waiting for or undergoing treatment which could give them a baby. One in three say that their relationship with their partner is weaker as a result of failing to conceive. (This statistic actually encourages me, though, because it means that two thirds of these couples have not fallen prey to the stress and anxiety of infertility, but have worked through some very difficult issues as couples.)

The above statistics were provided by the National Infertility Awareness Campaign, which seeks to ensure that infertile couples receive the medical help that they need. Their address and telephone number can be found at the back of the book, along with those of other counselling and support groups.

There are many misconceptions and old wives' tales about infertility, partly because we do not talk about it enough. There are a couple of these which are guaranteed to get me angry; mainly because they display such a lack of thought on the part of the speaker. You may find it hard to believe that people really say these things but let me assure you, they do.

Number one in this hit list is 'All you have to do is relax. Put it all out of your mind and let nature take its course.' If only it were so simple. Rape victims who have become pregnant as a result of being attacked know that relaxing has nothing to do with it. How will relaxing unblock a woman's fallopian tubes or increase a man's sperm count? This type of comment just loads guilt onto the childless, because it somehow then becomes your fault that you aren't getting pregnant. If there was anything that I could do to improve my chances of conceiving, don't you think that I would have tried it?

Having said that, it is easier said than done to try and relax when you are in the middle of this sort of emotional turmoil. The people who tell you that you just need to relax are often the same people who also put lots of pressure on you by asking the awkward questions. They don't always make it easy for you to relax.

A favourite comment is that I should get myself a child substitute, and somehow this will allow my mothering instincts to come to the fore and persuade my physical body to catch up with my mind and emotions. Much as I love dogs, I do not believe that looking after a puppy would change my situation in any way. This type of comment is really just another version of the 'You only need to relax' syndrome.

Taking the substitute argument one stage further, we have been told that it's a great idea for us to adopt, because that will somehow then free me to become pregnant and have a child of my own. I have been told numerous stories of people who did just this. Even if this is true (which I doubt), I have several problems with this: how do you think the adopted child feel may feel, if there is any suggestion that they are just there to enable someone else to come on the scene? Somebody once told me that this would make the adopted child feel very special, because they had been so useful. I beg to differ. I think that this would be the quickest way to make someone feel rejected, second-class and used – to be told that they are not valuable in their own right, but only because of what they could do for someone else. I don't think that we would have got through the adoption approval procedure if the social workers had thought that we were adopting just to give ourselves a greater chance of having our own children.

Another assumption that some people make is that there must be something wrong with your sex life if you can't have children. It's as though we only need to work on the correct technique, or learn how to do it properly (and we have been given advice on this before!) and all our problems will be solved. I'm not sure quite where this attitude comes from, but I can't imagine ever trying to give anyone that sort of advice, especially if they hadn't asked me for it. What is it in some people that they cannot resist trying to solve another person's problem?

It is interesting to note that it always seems to be me who gets the advice and comments, rather than Jon. I'd like to think that this is because I am seen as the more approachable one, but I know that's not true. I suspect it has more to do with the fact that infertility is still seen as a woman's issue. Whichever one of us is infertile, we are both affected by it equally. We, as a couple, cannot have children, and we both have to come to terms with that and its effects on our lives.

Chapter 4

How Can Other Christians Help?

The information blurb about a Christian author or speaker invariably includes something along the lines of 'Adam Jones lives in Eden-by-the-River with his wife, Eve, and their three children.' On one level, this can be useful information; it helps us to understand the context from which he may be speaking or writing. However, it seems to me that there can also be a sub-text, which goes like this: 'You can trust Adam Jones. He's normal. He fits into the Christian sub-culture.' Before you dismiss this as the ravings of a bitter woman, think about the adverts for ministers' jobs which ask for a 'family' man. The assumption is that this type of person will be well-balanced and adjusted – and so, by implication, someone who doesn't fit the stereotype may not be.

I realise that this could be the subject of another book, but some fellowships give the impression that only families with children are welcome. Family services are too often seen as services for children, rather than the whole church family. I think that Paul is serious when he tells us that we all belong to one body and, in our diversity, we need each other (1 Corinthians 12:12–31). By that, I mean that we all need each other as we are, not fitted into the mould that the church can sometimes create for us.

We love to categorise people so that we feel comfortable with them. How do the elderly, the childless, the single, the divorced, the single parents, those who don't match up to the safe 'Christian' ideal, fit into your scheme of things? I know of people who will not go to a family service because they feel that their personal circumstances don't come up to scratch. It's not necessarily that anyone ever vocalises these things, but attitudes come across, even when nothing is said. Let me give you a personal example:

Have you ever thought how difficult it is for someone like me to sit through a Mothering Sunday service? Everything about such a service just reinforces my disappointment (on a good day) or my pain and anguish (on a bad day). I know that some churches try and avoid any potential difficulties by ensuring that every adult female is given some flowers, but it can be very hard to sit and wait to be remembered as an afterthought, while others around you are surrounded by flowers. Some churches don't even make this concession to pastoral sensitivity, and I have been in services when those women without children present (whether elderly, divorced, single or childless) are ignored completely or literally given the dregs when all the 'proper' women have received their flowers. In my unregenerate stubbornness, I make myself go to these services every year, mainly so that people won't comment on my absence, but I don't find it easy.

Perhaps I am over-sensitive, but the message I get from a Mothering Sunday service is that I don't really count or am somehow a second-class woman, and I know that some single women feel the same way. Is this a situation where the 'weaker brother' principle ought to apply? Maybe those women who are fortunate enough to have children, and to have good ongoing relationships with those children, should think about forgoing their yearly celebration in church. Not because there is anything wrong in celebrating motherhood, but because it can be so painful for others. I don't just mean those who are childless either, but also those who have fallen out with their children or parents and live totally separate lives from them (this is more common in Christian circles than you may think), those who have been severely disappointed by parenthood, or those who don't see their children any more because of divorce.

There is a lot of pressure in society for people to have children. It is seen as the normal, acceptable thing to do.

People very rarely question you or your motives for having children, but they have hundreds of questions if you don't. Let me just say that questions like 'Whose fault is it?' are really not going to help the person you're asking. For one thing, in a significant number of cases, there is no clear answer to that question. Even if there is a 'guilty party', for both the man and the woman the inability to have children strikes at the very heart of what it can mean to be masculine or feminine. Low self-esteem and guilt are old friends to those who feel that they have failed others' expectations. They don't need to be reminded of their perceived failure.

I would like to be able to say that I haven't found this type of attitude in the church; but in my experience, Christians often seem to take society's values on board without thinking about whether they are biblical or merely cultural. In fact, the only really negative experiences I have had have been at the hands of Christians. I'm sure that most of them were well-meaning, but that really is no excuse for displaying a complete lack of awareness and sensitivity, particularly from those who knew about our situation.

I think that I was first asked the inevitable question, 'When are you going to start a family?' about three months after we got married. At the time it was easy to handle and a bit of a joke but, when we realised that we might not be able to have our own children, answering that question became very painful. At first, I gave the impression that we weren't ready to think about having children, but this becomes harder to do as time goes on. It can also lead to some lectures on your duties and responsibilities as a wife. There have been times when I have been harangued in church (only by one or two people, admittedly) – in a very 'loving' way, of course – and told that I am being selfish for thinking about my career and not giving Jon children. Are other personal and sensitive areas discussed with such a lack of thought and consideration, or is it just this one?

I have found that Christians often find it more difficult than non-Christians to accept that you can have a fulfilling life without children. I'm sure this is partly because I studied and worked amongst women who had ambitions in life other than raising a family, but I think that there is more to it than that. It is accepted in parts of our society that there are many different ways of living a fulfilling life – but I have come across Christians who simply do not believe that anyone can be content or complete without children.

I believe that God calls us to be at peace with him and with ourselves; and part of this is accepting that we may not get everything we want in life, whether this is children or anything else. If we can only be happy when we have everything we want, then we are allowing no room for God – we are relying on finding happiness or contentment in our possessions or our surroundings, not in God's love. Paul could honestly say that everything he had was rubbish compared to knowing God (Philippians 3:8). We preach that in our churches, but do we show it in the way that we live and the things that we expect of others?

Is this problem partly a throwback to the idea that childlessness is a sign of God's curse; something that shouldn't happen to a Christian who is following God's will? I hope that one of the things I do in this book is to suggest that simplistic conclusions very rarely meet the needs of a situation. The biblical examples I mention show clearly that some people are childless in spite of living righteous and blameless lives. Yes, it is helpful to look at our lives and the ways in which we may have opened ourselves up to malign influences, but this is not the whole answer for everybody.

I have been very hurt in the past by some thoughtless comments that people have made. Judgements have been given on my relationship with God, assumptions have been made about my past and present behaviour – all given in the name of being helpful and spiritual. People I hardly know have come up to me and given some very explicit advice about what Jon and I should be doing to have children. If anyone ever tells me again that I just need to relax, then I shan't be responsible for my actions!

I have found that Christians can be very quick to give advice and very slow to listen. I know that I am generalising and I want to put on record again that Jon and I have been very blessed by the Christians who have helped us through the hard times, and those who have given us enough space to allow God to heal us, rather than trying to do it themselves. I recognise now that the inappropriate reactions and help that we have been on the receiving end of stem from the difficulty that some people have with our situation. There is a need in some people to try and solve things for us. There also seems to be a cultural rather than spiritual reaction to our childlessness – it is against the natural order of things, it's not what society expects and we are therefore to be pitied.

The impression given is that the only way that we can become normal in the sight of the church is by having children. It was an immense relief to me when I realised that I wasn't letting God down (or anyone else, for that matter) by not bearing children. Children are a gift, not an automatic part of life – my life is not meaningless because I haven't given birth to children. God can and will use me in all sorts of ways, and this is not a second-class option just for those of us who haven't made it to the best way of living.

The unspoken message in some churches is that those who are single or childless must be labouring under massive disappointments. Some of us are, but it is possible to be single or childless and know that you are a complete person in God's eyes – you are not missing anything or living under a cloud. I have even heard Christians say that Jesus would have been a more complete person if he had been married and had children. What arrogance, and blasphemy! If the most complete person who ever lived does not fit the stereotype that the church proclaims, then is it possible that there may be something wrong with the stereotype?

What does the Bible teach us about families? Again, this is really the subject of another book, but it seems to me that the nuclear family ideal that is held in high esteem in some Christian circles is primarily cultural rather than biblical. In the Old Testament, there is no specific word for family, in the sense of meaning father, mother and children. A much more common concept is that of house or household; which can mean those living under the same roof whether biologically related or not, an extended family or an entire nation.

The concept is similar in the New Testament, and very little of Jesus' teaching or the New Testament letters are on the subject of the importance of the nuclear family. I'm not saying, though, that the Bible considers the family to be a trivial matter. Obviously, the Bible does stress the importance of a cohesive family in the commandment to honour our fathers and mothers, as well as the call to fidelity within marriage and sexual abstinence outside marriage.

The Bible is full of people doing God's work and, for some of these, their marital status or details of their offspring are not known. Clearly, it is irrelevant information. How do we judge people? By their job, family, or financial situation? Do we look at the heart as God does, or do we look at their external circumstances?

I think that what I am getting round to saying is that the church should be a place where people can be real with each other. Where the wounded can come to be patched up, those who are weary of life can be refreshed and restored, those who need comfort can find it, and those who feel that life offers no hope, can meet the source of all hope. If our churches give out the message that we have to conform to an ideal to be acceptable, then we have missed the point of the Gospel altogether. Jesus reserved his harshest criticism for those who thought that they had life sewn up, all the answers neatly ticked. Life can be difficult and messy for all of us in different sorts of ways – we mustn't exclude anyone from our fellowships because they don't fit in with our preferred lifestyle. Jesus never did that.

I don't really want to finish this chapter on a negative note – although I would hope that what I have said could be seen as a challenge rather than just criticism. As this chapter is all about the role that the church can play in helping people through difficult times, I also want to record some of my more positive experiences.

There are those in our current church fellowship who have quietly kept an eye on Jon and me and prayed for us, without asking lots of questions or forever asking for progress reports. They have made allowances for my bad moods and lack of communication without making a big deal out of it. Jon and I both feel loved and cared for by our church friends on the whole. For example, last Mothering Sunday, someone quickly noticed that I had not received any flowers and made sure that I got some before it became obvious. It didn't take away my discomfort with the service as a whole, but it did mean that I didn't have to deal with other people's reactions at a time when I felt vulnerable.

About a year after I started talking to Jackie about our situation, I felt it was right to tell the church as a whole. Jon would like to have done this earlier, but I wasn't sure that I could cope with everyone knowing about something which seemed so personal – I wasn't sure that I could handle their reactions and comments. Anyway, after thinking and praying about it for a couple of months, I was sure that it was the right thing to do. One evening service I got up, shaking like a leaf, and gave my testimony. I'm not sure what the congregation were expecting, but it wasn't a traditional sort of testimony. I didn't tell them about all the usual things and I didn't give them a story with a nice ending. I tried to explain how I felt and what I thought God was teaching me through the experience. It was all based around Psalm 13, which means an awful lot to me. In this psalm, David cries out to God about how he feels abandoned and forgotten – but while he is still in that situation, David can say that he trusts God and praises him for the good things that he has done in his life.

After the service, I braced myself for the reaction. I did get a lot of comments; some of surprise, some of sorrow, some sharing their own experiences. I was aware that I may be on the receiving end of pity and over-the-top sentimentality, but I was pleasantly surprised on the whole. One person simply said 'Well done. That must have been a really difficult thing for you to do' – a reaction that I would not have expected from them. That evening, I learnt the important lesson that your worst fears are not always realised; people can surprise you in good ways, as well as bad ways.

Jon and I experienced another positive reaction from a Christian friend some months later, when we had suffered a big disappointment. I thought that I didn't want to talk to anyone about it at the time, I was too busy being upset. Jon needed to talk to someone quickly, though, and rang the first person who came to mind – a lady in our church who he had been sharing with the previous day. She just said how sorry she was and that she didn't know what else to say. Ten minutes later she was on the doorstep. Before she came in, she told us that if this was the last thing we wanted or needed, then she would go away. We invited her in and she hugged us both and let us talk. She only stayed a few minutes, but her intervention was spot on. We needed to know that we mattered to someone and she proved that by her actions. Thanks, Mavis.

About a year ago, I met a couple who have been involved in the healing ministry for many years – Ruth and Joe Hawkey. They came to lead a prayer ministry weekend at our church, and I was slightly nervous because they were going to stay with us. (It was my own fault that I was in this position because I had invited them to come to our church after hearing them do a series of seminars.) Anyway, I couldn't work out how I was going to avoid the subject of children for a whole weekend and, if the subject came up, how would they react to our childlessness? Were they going to want to pray for us in a way that meant going over old ground yet again? I needn't have worried. They were very easy to talk to and didn't make any of the blunders that I have talked about earlier in the book. Since then, I have talked to them about all sorts of issues in my life, and their concern and love has been a real privilege to experience. I hope they won't mind me saying that I think of them almost as an extra set of parents.

I'm not going to try and list all the times when I have been touched by people's consideration and care, but it really makes a difference to know that there are people who care and want the best for you. Jon and I have been given a lot of love and space in our current parish. The times when I have felt unable to let my true feelings show have been largely because of my own insecurities, not because our church has imposed a pattern of expected behaviour on me.

Chapter 5

My Relationship with God

I realise that I've written quite a lot about how other people have helped or hindered me in my coming to terms with being childless, but there is another aspect to all this – and that is how my relationship with God has developed over the years: how he has helped me to reach a point of acceptance about being childless and enabled me to face up to other issues in my life; how my personality and spirituality have been factors, and what emotions I have gone through at different stages of the whole process. This will probably be the hardest chapter for me to write, because it will mean trying to being honest with myself and facing up to aspects of myself that I don't always like or find easy.

I have been a Christian since I was fourteen, and my view of God has changed dramatically over the years. I know that I can only have a partial view of God at the moment (the same as any other human being), but I do feel that I know God better now than I did then.

When I first became a Christian, I thought that God was like a favourite teacher – someone that you wanted to please, but who would be disappointed in you if you didn't achieve your potential. I thought that I had to try and get things right for God, to work hard to earn his praise, and that I had to be careful not to make mistakes. Inevitably, I did get things wrong (and obviously I still do) and I have had to learn that, if God can forgive me, then I need to be able to forgive myself. This has not been an easy lesson for me to learn, partly because I don't think I really understood the concept of forgiveness at all when I started out as a Christian. There were times when I thought that I had completely blown it with God and that there was no way back for me. I have been so hard on myself in the past that I have found it difficult to accept that God will not give up on me at some stage.

This view of God became significant and important when I was trying to deal with being childless. It encouraged me to keep looking back at the past to see where I had gone wrong – to search out the past sin, weakness or disobedience which would explain why I couldn't have children. My thinking was that I must have let God down somewhere along the line or none of this would be happening. God must be disappointed in me for some reason, and this was one way for him to show it. This became a very destructive way of thinking for me – or rather it always had been destructive, I just hadn't seen its significance before. The reactions of some Christians around me didn't help in this respect either, because they would just tend to reinforce the view that there must be some key in the past that I wasn't dealing with.

Over a couple of years, God began to show me that he isn't an authority figure in the way that I had perceived him to be. The Bible verses that I seemed to be guided to were more to do with God as comforter and sustainer, than judge and teacher. I began to realise that God wasn't outside the situation looking in, judging my performance and reactions, but he was in the middle of it all with me. He was sharing all the pain, frustration, disappointment, grief and anger – and I gradually began to understand that I didn't have to apologise for all these feelings or pretend that they weren't there.

Someone once said (I don't know who to attribute this to) that God is never disillusioned with us, because he never had any illusions about us in the first place. I needed to learn that God could see right through my pretence and the way that I tried to create an image of myself, to try and please him and others. He could see the real me inside, but he didn't think any the less of me as a result. When you really let that truth take root inside you, it transforms the way you think of yourself and others. I don't have to behave in a particular way or achieve anything to be acceptable to God; I just have to be who God wants me to be, the person he created me to be – whatever that means in my particular case. I'm not saying that I have fully grasped the immensity of God's love for me, but I have begun to experience it and I know that God will help me to take hold of that truth and live in it, if I let him.

As I began to understand that God was sharing the whole experience with Jon and me, I realised that my view and perceptions of God had been sadly lacking. There were no tests to pass or expectations to meet, God just wanted me to be real and honest with him – to let him in so that he could help me to understand and deal with the emotions that kept flooring me. Initially, I thought I should do this so that God could take those feelings away, but I now realise that he's not going to do that, and that it wouldn't be a solution if he did. God is an emotional God. Jesus showed this in his life – the only difference between us and him is that Jesus always had appropriate emotions. His weeping, anger, joy and compassion were genuine and sincere, but always fitting. Our sin and brokenness can mean that our reactions and emotions are sometimes out of place, but that doesn't mean that we live better Christian lives by denying their existence.

Part of the problem for me was that I didn't always understand where the feelings were coming from. I have heard and read that other childless people have the same sort of experience – you can't always explain why you feel the way you do, you just know that the feelings hit you at the very heart of your being, sometimes when you least expect them. It's hard to describe; it's like being hit by a bombshell, and you don't always know what will start the reaction off. This can be true for people who don't even think that they are particularly bothered about having children – sometimes the fact that they will be childless for life can just hit home, even at the most inopportune or unlikely time.

Some situations are obviously going to be difficult for people like Jon and me; such as baptisms, or family celebrations that are dominated by children. But these don't always cause me a problem because I can get myself 'geared up' to cope. It's as though the defences go up and I devise a coping strategy, which means that my primary aim is self-protection. I have found that I can switch off in these situations until after the event, but this usually only postpones the feelings; it doesn't allow me to ignore them or avoid them completely. It's when the emotions catch you unawares, or a situation arises that you haven't anticipated, that the problems can really start. There have been times when I have stopped in the middle of a bout of tears and said 'Where on earth did that come from?' I know now that it's better for me to concentrate on getting the emotions out rather than worrying too much about where they came from. I rationalise things far too much and this is something that you can't always be rational or logical about. I am learning how important it is to go with the flow and just admit to my feelings, but it doesn't come naturally to me at all. I find it very difficult to let my feelings show when there are other people around (with one or two exceptions), and this has been a real barrier for me.

One of the feelings that I have found it hardest to admit to is grief. I have felt very guilty for grieving, because the grief seemed so intangible and unreasonable. I would always think that there were other people who had been through so much more, or lost much more than me. How could I be grieving when there was no person to grieve for? It was just another month that I hadn't got pregnant. The grief can be soul-destroying, though, because there is no way that you can get it in perspective. There is no person, time or place to focus on and the wounds are re-opened every month, so there is no way that time can play a healing role – the intensity of the feelings comes back over and over again. The times when I was undergoing fertility treatment were the worst in this respect.

It sounds like a bit of a cliché if I say that God has comforted me and brought me through all this grief, but that's the truth of it. He has surrounded me with comfort and support and allowed me to take my time in dealing with the things that have troubled me. For as long as I have been a Christian, I have always known (in my head) that God is with me and I have found great security in that. Now, though, I can feel that God's presence is with me in a way that I never did before and I have the assurance of knowing that his arms are around me and he is always close to me. I can say that I don't feel as though I am grieving any more, but I couldn't say that there is never any sadness.

Anger is another emotion that I have experienced but have found it difficult to voice. I find it hard to admit to feeling anger because I have thought that being angry puts me automatically in the wrong. It has taken me a while to realise that anger is not something that you always have to apologise for – it is a natural reaction, and trying to hide it only makes the feelings stronger. It is easy to mask anger and call it something else, but you don't resolve it that way.

I have been very angry about being childless. It can seem so unfair that some people are having unwanted children or abortions, while there are others who would love to have children, but can't. There seems to be no correlation between your ability to conceive and your potential parenting skills – surely God should arrange it so that children are born to those who can cope and those who will love and nurture their offspring? Reality shows us that this isn't the case.

My anger can come out in various ways: I have reacted badly to news stories of child abuse or other situations where children have not received the protection that is their due. I get easily irritated and annoyed by parents who complain or constantly moan about their children, or those who seem to care more about themselves than their offspring. I can have a very sharp tongue (sarcasm is a great defence mechanism for me) and I have used it to lash out at those who have hurt me; as well as those who haven't, but who were just unlucky enough to catch me at a bad time.

I have found it helpful to consider what I am actually feeling angry about. I usually feel myself getting irritable or angry without being able to admit to or sometimes knowing, what the real issues are. I'm very good at projecting the anger onto someone or something that isn't as painful, so that I don't have to work through the hard things that are really the problem. Now I realise that I do that, I am beginning to be able to deal with it.

Again, God has shown me that anger in the right place is OK, as long as I deal with it and don't let it fester. I've also learnt that God is big enough to cope with my anger and that he doesn't mind me unloading it all onto him. In fact, he would far rather I did that than keep it all to myself and pretend that there is no anger there. I used to think that Christians shouldn't be angry and so, when I felt anger, I had to try and hide it or I thought I would be letting God down. This all goes back to my original view of God as someone who I didn't want to be disappointed in me.

Depression is another common emotion in someone who would love to have children, but can't. As I said in an earlier chapter, the vast majority of those who go through fertility treatment encounter depression to a greater or lesser extent at some stage. One in five even contemplates suicide. I think this is partly because of the isolation that may surround you, even though this can be self-imposed.

I have been very fortunate, in that I have had the support of Jon, our families and friends; but I recognise now that, in the past, I have experienced some of the milder symptoms of depression – inability to concentrate, disturbed sleep patterns, and low energy levels. However good the support around you is, there can be times when it feels as though nobody understands you and that there is no-one who can relate to your pain. This is where knowing God has been my bedrock. I know that he understands me and shares everything that I've gone through. Isaiah 43 has been a very important passage of the Bible for me over many years, and it reminds me of the way that God is our protector and comforter – always there for us:

> *'Fear not, for I have redeemed you;*
>   *I have called you by name; you are mine.*
> *When you pass through the waters,*
>   *I will be with you;*
> *and when you pass through the rivers,*
>   *they will not sweep over you.*

> When you walk through the fire,
>   you will not be burned;
>   the flames will not set you ablaze.
> For I am the Lord, your God,
>   the Holy One of Israel, your Saviour . . . '

(Isaiah 43:1b–3a)

The Psalms have come to mean a lot to me as well. There are so many examples in them of God being present in every aspect of our lives, the good and the bad. As I've said before, Psalm 13 is a particular favourite because it doesn't pull any punches. David says exactly how he feels about a terrible situation, but he doesn't just stay with that; he reflects on God's character too. David knows that God is faithful and that his love is constant and unconditional; even if he doesn't always feel as though this is the case.

At the times when I have felt down, it has helped me to know that God thinks that my life is worthwhile. I am going somewhere, there is a purpose to my life, there is a point to it all.

This has been particularly important to me when I have felt a failure and the sense of disappointment with my life has become overwhelming. The feelings of unfulfilled hopes and lost dreams can really bear down on the childless. Denial of your situation gradually turns into frustration and despair, as you realise that you may never possess something that you consider to be very important. You feel helpless and realise that there is nothing that you can do to change the situation – something a control freak like me finds it almost impossible to come to terms with.

The uncertainty of it all is the most difficult thing to bear. It is very hard to come to terms with being childless, because every month there is the hope that your situation may change. It's almost like the addicted gambler who always thinks that the next bet will be the one that makes his fortune; and then the next, and the next . . . . Letting go of your hopes and dreams is like giving up on the only way out of your situation that you can see. Like the gambler, I didn't realise that, for me, hanging on to the hopes and dreams of having a child was just dragging me down further.

God says that his grace is sufficient for us – that it is in our weakness that his power is made perfect (2 Corinthians 12:9). For a long time, I thought that I had to be strong and not give up – I honestly thought that was what God would expect of me. I now realise that God has been able to work more through my weakness and vulnerability than he ever could when I was still trying to keep going and stay strong. Having said this, I still find it very hard not to go back to my old ways of putting up the defences and trying to cope with everything on my own. I know that I have to be careful when I feel strong, because this is when I tend to shut God out and try and handle everything by myself.

I started this chapter by saying that I used to think of God as a favourite teacher, and that my experiences (and God's patient prompting) have caused my views to change. The image that I have of God now, among others, is that of a good, loving parent with a toddler. When the child falls over or hurts themselves, a good parent doesn't say to them that they feel let down or disappointed – they rush over to pick the child up, dust them down and help them to get back on their feet. The toddler doesn't have to achieve anything stupendous to be praised and loved – most parents seem to be ridiculously pleased with even the smallest thing that a child does. God looks at us like that – we're not always being given marks out of ten, but he regards us with affection, love and compassion.

Like other good parents, God will put us right when we go wrong, but he doesn't condemn us or bear grudges. He really wants the best for us and he is the best judge of what that is. God wants me to build a relationship of love and trust with him – not one of fear, distance and duty-driven respect.

I have come to a point now where I know that I can never blow it with God. He will always be there to pick me up when I fall over, if I let him.

Chapter 6

Conclusion –

(God Is Healing Me)

I believe that God heals, and that he could 'heal' me now and give me a child. I have struggled in the past with why he hasn't done this. To a large extent, I have stopped looking for the key that will solve it all for me, and asked God to be Lord in my life and to do what he wants in me. If that sounds a bit glib, then I'm sorry – it's not glib, or easy. For a long time, I tried to tell God what he should be doing for me, and I must have really exasperated him sometimes. I know now that he has all sorts of things for me if I will only shut up and let him speak. As I said in the introduction, I have learnt that God's view of my need for healing may well be different to mine; and I won't get very far if I refuse to look at what his will for me might be.

I've got to the stage now where I don't mind if some other Christians think that I'm running away from my problem. Contrary to some people's opinions, giving birth to a child is not the only solution to the problem of childlessness. Some people will look at adopting, others will discover that their lives can be fulfilled without raising children. God is a God of infinite variety and he deals with us as individuals. We need to share our lives with him and listen to him, not tell him what we want from him.

I know that God has the best for us and I know that he's guiding us. Jon and I are sure that it's right for us to adopt – to give a Christian home to a child or children who wouldn't otherwise have known that security – and it may be that we wouldn't have listened to God in this respect if we had been given our own children. As to the future; if God decides to give us a child that is biologically ours as well, then we're open to that. We're not shutting the door on the possibility that I may give birth to a child or children, we just don't feel that this is the main issue any more. Our lives are made complete in God, not in anything else.

I don't believe that God enjoys seeing anyone go through pain and suffering of whatever kind, but I do believe that he can bring good things out of a situation. He's enabled me to change through this experience in ways that I never dreamed possible.

I have always been a very self-sufficient person, never able to ask for help, and until I hit this barrier of childlessness I intended to keep it that way. I found that I couldn't handle this situation on my own and I needed someone other than Jon to help me. Jon and I seemed to drag each other down at times; we would get depressed about things at different stages and we seemed to force each other into an extreme positive or negative state just to counterbalance the other one's views.

As I said earlier, I opened up to a friend, Jackie, and told her the whole story. This was a huge risk for me, as I had a great fear of being let down by people that I trusted. Over the coming months, she became a lifesaver for me – someone to moan at and to share the emotional roller-coaster that is fertility treatment. Care and support like that is invaluable. If you've ever experienced it, you'll know what I mean. But, please don't offer help like that unless you're willing and able to see it through. If Jackie had got bored with my moaning, or lost interest in Jon and me and our situation, then I would have been worse off than if she'd never got involved.

As well as discovering how great a commitment and support real friendship can be, I began to grasp the fact that some people can be trusted. My habit has been to treat everybody with suspicion – never giving the benefit of the doubt to anyone, just in case they let me down. Having discovered that it was possible to take the risk of sharing yourself with others, I began to open up on other issues in my life. This is a very slow, painful and ongoing process and one that I may not have started had I known the full extent of it back on that Sunday evening when I talked to Jackie for the first time.

It has been a tough time, and I'm glad that a lot of the hard work is behind me now. It was definitely worth it, though, because I can honestly say that the last couple of years have changed my life immeasurably for the better as God has dealt with things that I have kept deeply hidden from everyone – and tried to hide from him. The catalyst in all of this for me was facing up to not having children and realising that there are some things in life that you can't cope with on your own.

I've recently read a book called *Some Mothers Do Have 'em, Others Don't* by Hugo and Sharon Anson. It's a very helpful book on infertility and childlessness, and there is one paragraph in there that says exactly what I'm trying to say here:

> 'So if you are feeling things that don't make sense, don't just push them away. Take time and learn about yourself. It may be the most important thing you ever do.'

I still find it difficult to trust people, but I know now that it can be worth taking the risk; and I also know that God will never rush you into healing. He takes things at a pace that you can handle – even if an arthritic snail could move faster! I've also been amazed at the things that are possible with God. Things that I thought were permanent fixtures in my life have been removed, though I am aware that there is still some more structural work needed.

We can live 'partial' Christian lives and limit God by saying that there are things that we are stuck with and cannot break free from, but God does not intend us to live like that. It can sometimes appear to be more comfortable to hang onto things that hold us back, but it doesn't have to be that way. Jesus came to give us abundant life, not a mediocre excuse for life.

Another thing that I have learnt is that God wants me to live the life he has actually given me, not spend my time waiting for something else to come along. You only get one life; seize the day and use what God has given you. Live the life he wants you to live, don't waste it.

I am a different person now from the one who moved to Runcorn four years ago. Perhaps it would be more correct to say that I am now more the person that God intended me to be. I would never have been able to write about my thoughts and feelings in this way before. I'm also glad that I gave up my job before moving here. The time that I have been able to spend thinking has been invaluable. I always used to run away from thinking, I tried to keep busy. God has used this time to help me to face up to a lot of difficult things, but so much that is positive has come out of it.

A little while ago, Ruth Hawkey had a picture from God about my life being changed. The way she described it was as a new painting being put on the wall of my life; a painting showing me as the person God created. Part of my struggle over the last few years has been to discover that the painting that I thought was me was not the real me at all. The person I thought I was or wanted to be, was not the person God created me to be. To a certain extent, we are all squashed or moulded by life in some way or another, and I had allowed other people's expectations and actions to alter me in ways that God did not intend.

I have had to allow God to remove the old painting, put the new one in its place and then move into living this new life so that the old view doesn't get put back on the wall again. It is so easy to slip back into old patterns of behaviour, particularly when the issues go very deep. I guess this is where sanctification comes in – the ongoing, long-term process.

God longs for us to let him put the pieces of our lives back together again. He is doing that in me and, because of this, I can say that giving birth to a child is no longer the issue for me that it once was.

A poem written by a friend sums up everything better than I could do myself, and I am grateful to Karen Vickers for allowing me to reproduce her poem.

'Shattered and Sunshined'

Imagine life as a huge sheet of glass – having many
colours, yet no order or form

Then it is   broken
and
     at
        that
            moment,
                 it feels disastrous
as though
       all is lost.

Imagine a master craftsman carefully, lovingly, picking
up each shard of glass and piecing them together to
create a beautiful stained glass window.

The coloured glass – lovelier than before
                          stronger than before
now fulfilling the purpose for which it was created.

A stained glass window – an object of beauty.
How much more beautiful though – when the light
     shines through.
An experience of brokenness ... of some years ago
Shattered but not obliterated.

Held – though oblivious to this at the time.

Only too aware, though, of the light around me
     afterwards
A total contrast to the previous darkness

Stronger than before

Brokenness producing wholeness.

Further Reading

I'm sure that there are other good books on the subject of childlessness that I haven't come across, but these are the ones that I have found helpful and challenging.

The Ache for a Child
Debra Bridwell, Victor Books

This book made a big impact on me, not always because I agreed with everything it said. The author managed to get me to admit to feelings that I had suppressed, even when I thought I was pretty well sorted. This is not always an easy book to read (I cried many times whilst reading it), but it may help those who know childless people to understand how they are feeling. The book's strong points include looking at how ethical and practical issues affect us emotionally, and how we need to deal with the very strong emotions that are around for childless people. This book covers miscarriage and infertility, including secondary infertility (when a couple have a child or children but are unable to have more).

Childless – The Hurt and the Hope
Beth Spring, Lion

This is a superb little booklet which could act as an introduction to the whole subject of infertility. In a very concise and clear way, it explores areas of pain, confusion, denial and anger. The author also has quite a lot to say on what makes a family and debunks some of the myths that seem to surround infertility.

Some Mothers Do Have 'em – Others Don't
Hugo and Sharon Anson, Eagle

This was the first helpful book that I found on the subject of infertility, and it was like a breath of fresh air to discover that other people had faced the same issues and prejudices as Jon and I. The authors carefully consider the various different options open to childless couples, including that of remaining childless. It is an honest book, and I particularly liked the sections which looked at why our feelings don't always make sense. Who said that we have to be rational about things like this?

When the Womb is Empty
Ray and Rebecca Larson, Whitaker House

It is worth getting this book just for the version of Psalm 139 which is included. (Gaye Ruschen considers the verses of the psalm from the infertile woman's point of view.)

The authors tell their own story, which is very moving in places, and they include a large section on adoption and pro-life activism – areas they moved into when their infertility was diagnosed. The sections on adoption are good from the emotional and spiritual standpoints, but not from the practical point of view because the authors are American and consequently are dealing with a very different system to our own.

Useful Addresses

National Infertility Awareness Campaign
PO Box 2106
London W1A 3DZ
Freephone: 0800 716345
Fax: 0171 437 0553

Child (Self-Help Network)
Charter House
43 St Leonard's Road
Bexhill-on-Sea
East Sussex TN40 1JA
Tel: 01424 732361
Fax: 01424 731858
e-mail: office@email2.child.org.uk
www: http://www.child.org.uk

Issue (The National Fertility Association)
509 Aldridge Road
Great Barr
Birmingham B44 8NA
Tel: 0121 344 4414

British Infertility Counselling Association
51 Queens Crescent
London NW5
Tel: 0171 354 3930

British Agencies for Adoption and Fostering
200 Union Street
London SE1 0LY

Tel: 0171 593 2000
Fax: 0171 593 2001